THE COMPLETE KEYBOARD PLAYER

CHART HITS OF THE 90s

WISE PUBLICATIONS
LONDON/NEW YORK/PARIS/SYDNEY/COPENHAGEN/MADRID

Exclusive Distributors:
MUSIC SALES LIMITED
8/9 Frith Street,
London W1V 5TZ, England.

MUSIC SALES PTY LIMITED
120 Rothschild Avenue,
Rosebery, NSW 2018,
Australia.

Order No. AM952622
ISBN 0-7119-7277-X
This book © Copyright 1998 by Wise Publications

Compiled by Peter Evans
Music arranged by Kenneth Baker
Cover design by Chloë Alexander
Photographs courtesy of London Features International

Printed in the United Kingdom by
Redwood Books Ltd, Trowbridge, Wilts.

YOUR GUARANTEE OF QUALITY
As publishers, we strive to produce every book to the highest
commercial standards.
This book has been carefully designed to minimise awkward page
turns and to make playing from it a real pleasure.
Particular care has been given to specifying acid-free, neutral-sized
paper made from pulps which have not been elemental chlorine
bleached. This pulp is from farmed sustainable forests and was
produced with special regard for the environment.
Throughout, the printing and binding have been planned to ensure a
sturdy, attractive publication which should give years of enjoyment.
If your copy fails to meet our high standards, please inform us and
we will gladly replace it.

Music Sales' complete catalogue describes thousands of titles
and is available in full colour sections by subject, direct from
Music Sales Limited. Please state your areas of interest and send
a cheque/postal order for £1.50 for postage to:
Music Sales Limited, Newmarket Road, Bury St. Edmunds,
Suffolk IP33 3YB.

Visit the Internet Music Shop at
http://www.musicsales.co.uk

ACHY BREAKY HEART

WORDS & MUSIC BY DON VON TRESS

Voice: jazz organ
Rhythm: rock
Tempo: medium (♩ = 128)

1. You can tell the world you ne-ver was my girl, you can burn my clothes up when I'm
2. You can tell your ma I moved to Ar-kan-sas, you can tell your dog to bite my

mf

gone. You can tell your friends just what a fool I've been, and
leg. Or tell your bro-ther Cliff, whose fist can tell my lip that he

laugh and joke a-bout me on the 'phone. You can tell my arms go
ne-ver real-ly liked me a-ny-way. Or tell your aunt Lou-ise, tell

back to the farm, you can tell my feet to hit the floor, or
an-y-thing you please, my-self al-read-y knows I'm not o-kay, or

you can tell my lips to tell my fin-ger tips they won't be reach-ing out for you no
you can tell my eyes to watch out for my mind, it might be walk-ing out on me to-

CHORUS

more. day.

But don't tell my heart, my a-chy, break-y heart, I

just don't think he'd un-der-stand. And if you tell my heart, my

a-chy, break-y heart,___ he might blow up and kill this man.

INSTRUMENTAL

guitar to organ

All For Love

WORDS & MUSIC BY BRYAN ADAMS, ROBERT JOHN 'MUTT' LANGE & MICHAEL KAMEN

Voice: brass ensemble
Rhythm: 8 beat
Tempo: quite slow ($\quarternote = 84$)

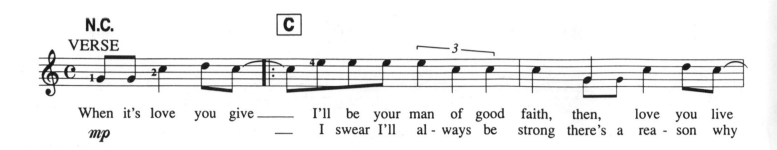

When it's love you give ___ I'll be your man of good faith, then, love you live
___ I swear I'll al-ways be strong there's a rea-son why

___ I'll make a stand, I won't blink, I'll be the rock you can build ___ on.
___ I'll prove to you we be-long, I'll be the one that pro-tects ___ you

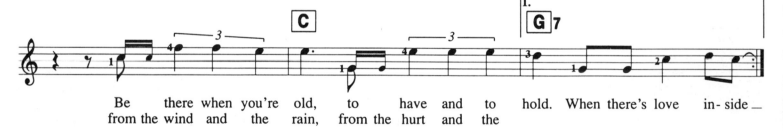

Be there when you're old, to have and to hold. When there's love in-side ___
from the wind and the rain, from the hurt and the

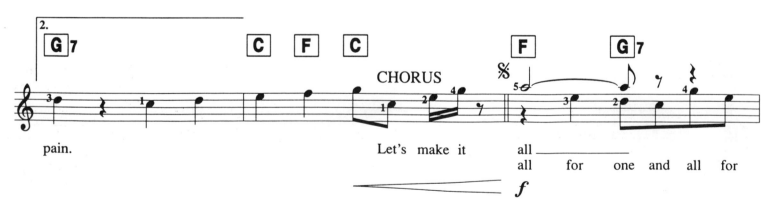

pain. Let's make it all ___
all for one and all for

love. Let the one you hold be the one you want, ___ the one you

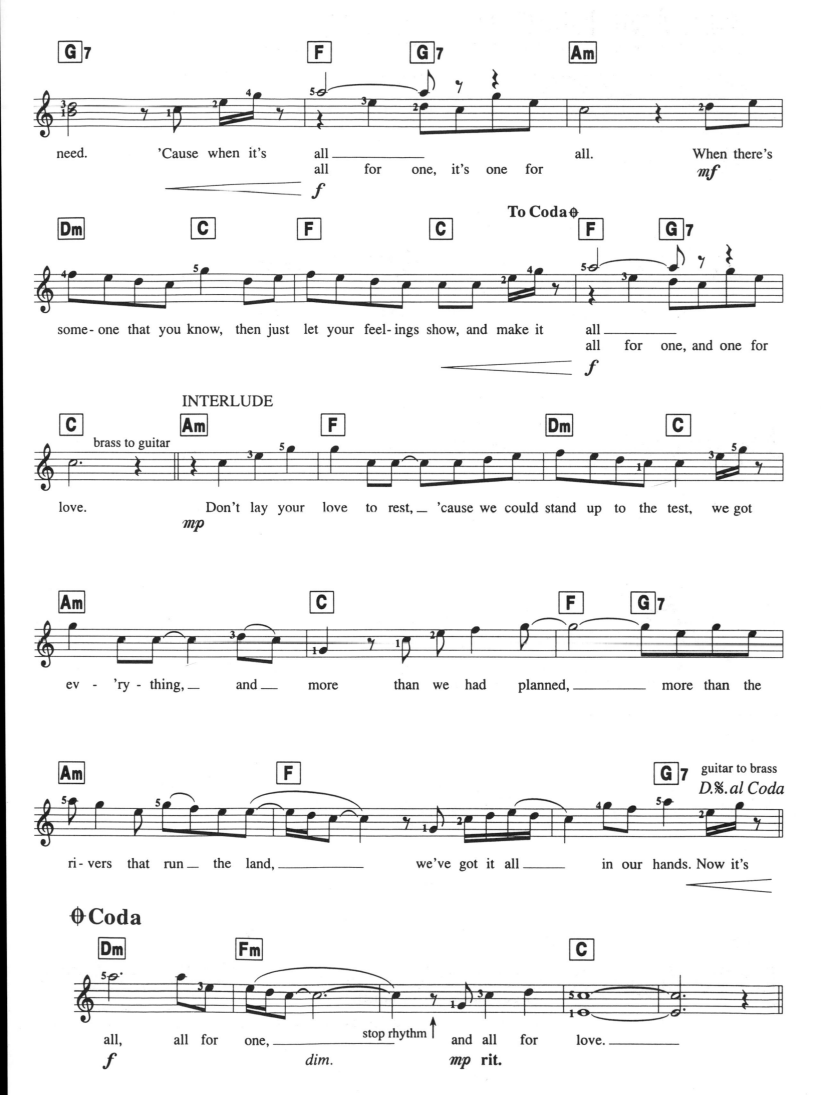

As Long As You Love Me
Words & Music by Max Martin

Voice: muted trumpet
Rhythm: 8 beat
Tempo: medium (♩ = 96)

VERSE

Al - though lone - li - ness has al - ways been a friend of mine, ___ I'm
how you got me blind is still a mys - te - ry, ___ I

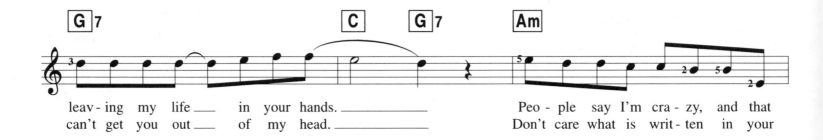

leav - ing my life ___ in your hands. ___ Peo - ple say I'm cra - zy, and that
can't get you out ___ of my head. ___ Don't care what is writ - ten in your

1.

I am blind, ___ risk - ing it all ___ in a glance. ___ And
his - to - ry, ___ as long as you're here ___ with me. ___

2.

CHORUS

to trumpet

___ I don't care who ___ you are, ___ where ___ you're from, ___ what ___

f

___ you did, ___ as long ___ as you love ___ me. Who ___ you are, ___ where ___

BLAZE OF GLORY

WORDS & MUSIC BY JON BON JOVI

Voice: guitar
Rhythm: rock
Tempo: medium (♩ = 100)

VERSES N.C. [Dm] [C] [G] [Dm] [F] [C]

1. I wake up in the morn-ing and I raise my wear-y head. I've got an
(2.) brought in-to this world, well they say you're born in sin. Well at
(3.) ask a-bout my con-science, and I of-fer you my soul. You ask if I'll

mp

old coat for a pil-low, and the earth was last night's bed. I
least they gave me some-thing I didn't have to steal, or have to win. They
grow to be a wise man, well I ask if I'll grow old. You

don't know where I'm go-ing, on-ly God knows where I've been, I'm a
tell me that I'm want-ed, yeah, I'm a want-ed man, I'm a
ask me if I've known love and what it's like to sing songs in the rain. Well I've

guitar to
brass ensemble
for CHORUS

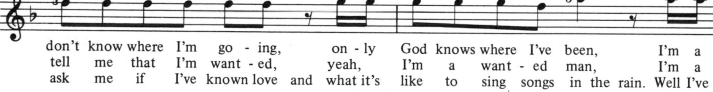

[G] [Dm]

de-vil on the run, a six-gun lo-ver, a can-dle in the wind. 2. When you're
colt in your sta-ble, I'm what Cain was to A-bel, catch me if you can I'm go-ing
seen love ___ come, I've seen it shot down, I've seen it die in vain. I'm go-ing

CHORUS

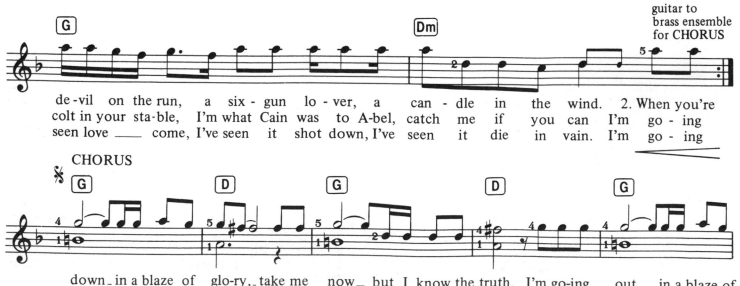

[G] [D] [G] [D] [G]

down_ in a blaze of glo-ry,_ take me now_ but I know the truth. I'm go-ing out _ in a blaze of

f

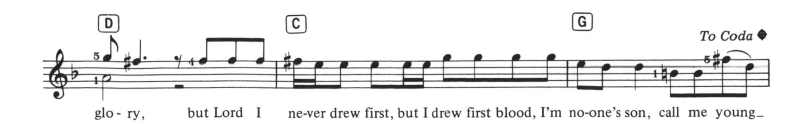

glo - ry,   but Lord I   ne-ver drew first, but I drew first blood, I'm no-one's son, call me young_

gun.   *dim.*   3. You

4. Each   night I   go   to bed, I pray the

mp

brasss to guitar

To Coda ◈

Lord my soul to keep, no I ain't look-ing for for-give-ness, but be - fore I'm six foot deep. Lord I

got to ask a fa-vour, and I   hope you'll   un-der-stand, 'cause I've   lived life to the full-est, let this

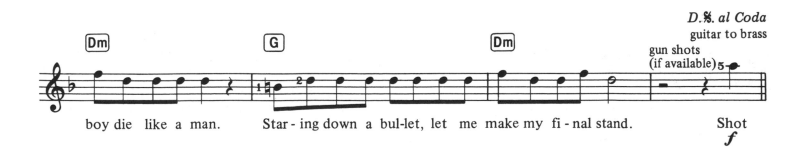

boy die   like a man.   Star - ing down a bul-let, let   me make my fi - nal stand.   Shot

f

D.S. al Coda
guitar to brass
gun shots
(if available)

gun,_____ call me young gun.___   Young

◈ *CODA*   *(Repeat and fade)*

11

CIRCLE OF LIFE (FROM WALT DISNEY PICTURES' "THE LION KING")

MUSIC BY ELTON JOHN | LYRICS BY TIM RICE

Voice: piano
Rhythm: 8 beat
Tempo: fairly slow (♩ = 88)

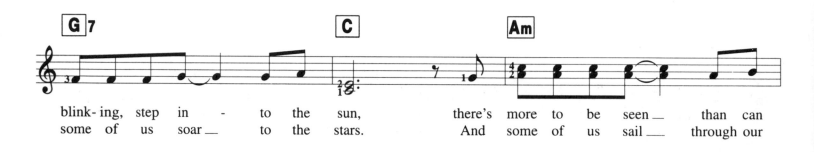

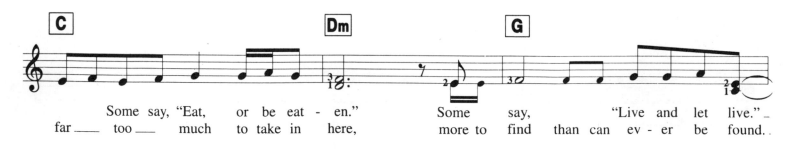

ne - ver take more — than you give in the cir - cle of life. }
small on the end - less — round, in the cir - cle of life. }
cresc.

mf

CHORUS

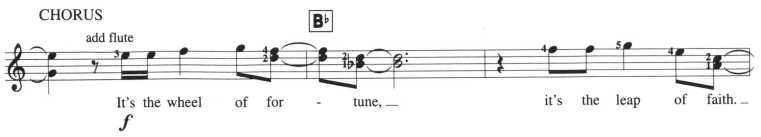

add flute

It's the wheel of for - tune, — it's the leap of faith. —

f

— It's the band — of hope, —

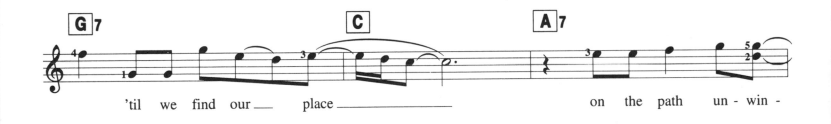

'til we find our — place on the path un - win -

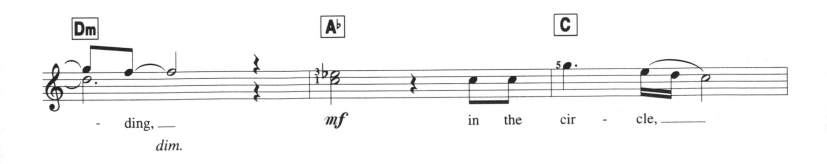

- ding, — in the cir - cle, —

dim.

mf

(Fine 2nd time)
cut flute

the cir - cle of life.

(stop rhythm
2nd time)

13

Don't You Love Me

WORDS & MUSIC BY CYNTHIA BIGGS, CAROLYN MITCHELL, TERENCE DUDLEY & CHRISTOPHER KELLUM

Voice: saxophone
Rhythm: rock
Tempo: medium (♩ = 92)

FATHER AND SON
WORDS & MUSIC BY CAT STEVENS

Voice: piano
Rhythm: 8 beat
Tempo: slow (♩ = 72)

1. It's not time to make a change, just re - lax, take it ea - sy, you're still

young, that's your fault, there's so much you have to know. Find a girl, set - tle down, if you want,

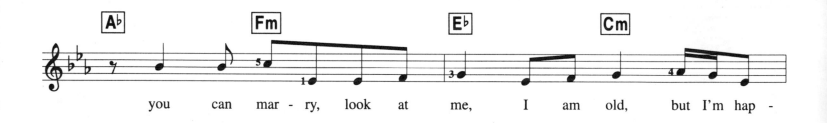

you can mar - ry, look at me, I am old, but I'm hap -

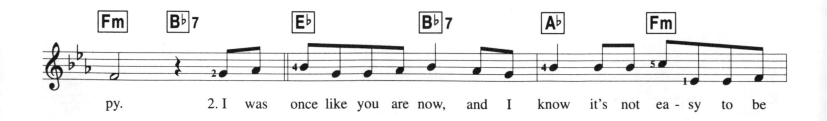

py. 2. I was once like you are now, and I know it's not ea - sy to be

calm, when you've found some - thing go - ing on. Take your

time,   think   a   lot,   think — of   ev - 'ry - thing   you've   got,   for   you   will

still   be   here   to   mor - row,   but   your   dreams   may   not.   3. How   can
mf

I   try   to   ex - plain?   When   I   do,   he   turns   a - way a - gain,   well,   it's
(4.) times   that   I   have   cried,   keep - ing   all   the   things   I   knew in - side,   and   it's

al - ways   been   the   same,   same   old   sto - ry.   From   the
hard, ___   but   it's   har - der   to   ig - nore   it.   If   they   were

mo - ment   I   could   talk,   I   was   or - dered   to   lis - ten,   there's   a
right ___   I'd   a - gree,   but   it's   them   they   know,   not   me,   now   there's   a

way, ____   and   I   know   that   I   have   to   go   a - way.   I
way, ____   and   I   know   that   I   have   to   go   a - way.   I
dim.

know   I   have   to   go.   4. All   the   go.
know   I   have   to   *mf*   stop rhythm
mp

17

GOODNIGHT GIRL

WORDS & MUSIC BY GRAEME CLARK, TOM CUNNINGHAM, NEIL MITCHELL & MARTI PELLOW

Voice: string ensemble
Rhythm: 8 beat
Tempo: medium (♩ = 100)

VERSES

1. You hear me ___ so clear - ly, ___ and see how ___ I
(2.) keep me ___ so near you, ___ and see me ___ so

try. You feel me, ___ so heal me, ___ and
far. And hold me, ___ and send me _____

tear me ___ a - part. And I won't tell a soul, ___
deep in ___ your heart. And I won't tell a soul, ___

_____ I won't ___ tell ___ at all, ___ and
_____ I won't ___ tell ___ at all, ___ and

do they have to know ___ *cresc.* a - bout my good - night girl.
I won't let them know ___ a - bout my good - night girl.

CHORUS

Caught up in your wish-ing well, your hopes in - side it, ___ take your love and pro-mis-

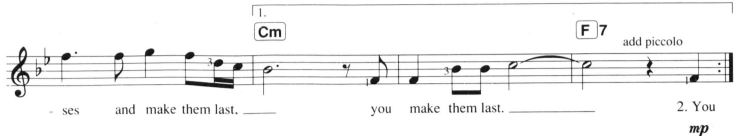

- ses and make them last, ___ you make them last. ___ 2. You

___ You make them last. ___ Caught up in your wish-ing well, your hopes in - side it, ___

take your love and pro-mi - ses and make them last, ___ you make them last. ___

INTERLUDE

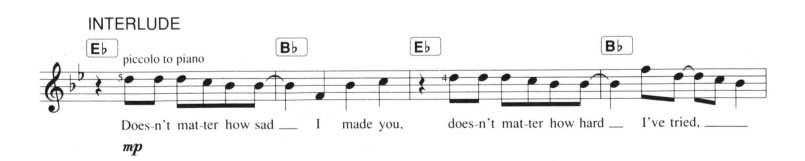

Does-n't mat-ter how sad ___ I made you, does-n't mat-ter how hard ___ I've tried, ___

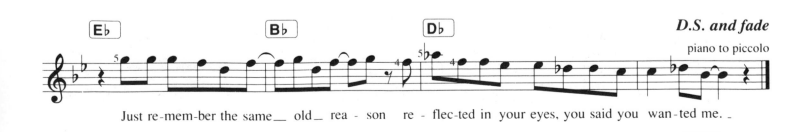

Just re-mem-ber the same ___ old ___ rea - son re - flec-ted in your eyes, you said you wan-ted me. ___

I Believe I Can Fly

Words & Music by Robert Kelly

Voice: vibraphone
Rhythm: 8 beat
Tempo: slow (♩ = 69)

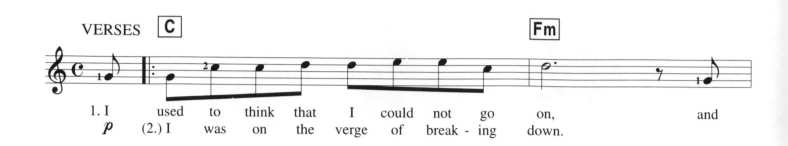

VERSES

1. I used to think that I could not go on, and
(2.) I was on the verge of break - ing down.

life was noth - ing but an aw - ful song. But now I know the mean - ing of true
some - times si - lence can seem so ____ loud. There are mi - ra - cles in life I must ach -

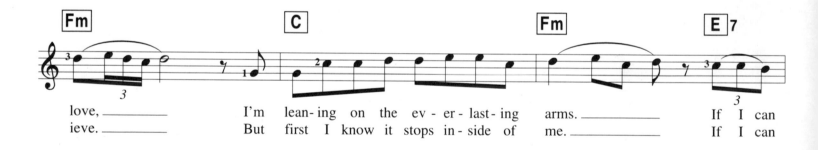

love, ____ I'm lean - ing on the ev - er - last - ing arms. ____ If I can
ieve. ____ But first I know it stops in - side of me. ____ If I can

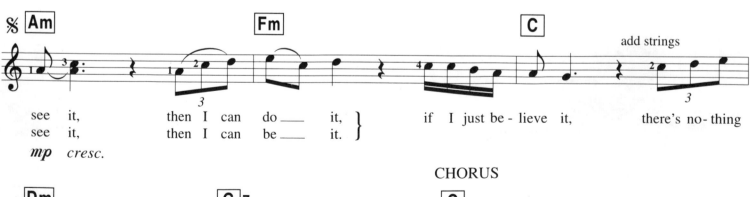

see it, then I can do ____ it, } if I just be - lieve it, there's no - thing
see it, then I can be ____ it. }

mp cresc.

CHORUS

to ____ it. I be - lieve I can fly. I be - lieve I can

f

I Will Always Love You
WORDS & MUSIC BY DOLLY PARTON

Voice: flute
Rhythm: 8 beat
Tempo: fairly slow (♩ = 80)

sweet me - mo - ries, that's all I am ta - king ___ with
hope life treats you kind, and I hope you have all that you e - ver

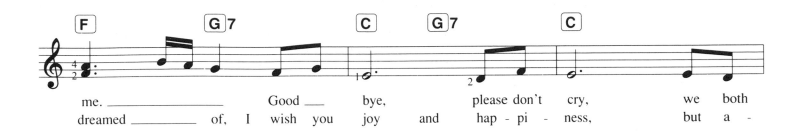

me. ___ Good ___ bye, please don't cry, we both
dreamed ___ of, I wish you joy and hap - pi - ness, but a -

CHORUS

add strings

know that I'm not ___ what you need, ___ but I ___ will
- bove all this I ___ wish you love, ___ *(Sing)* and I ___ will

f

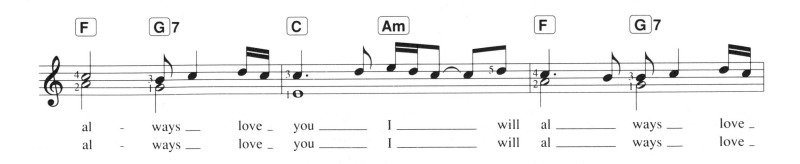

al - ways ___ love _ you ___ I ___ will al ___ ways ___ love _
al - ways ___ love _ you ___ I ___ will al ___ ways ___ love _

VERSE

1.   2.

cut strings

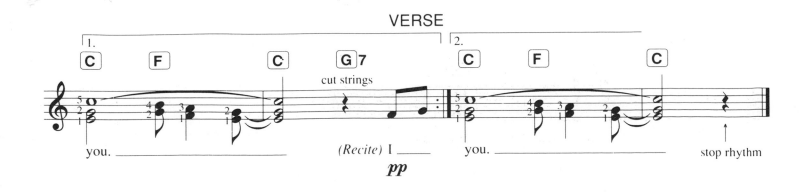

you. ___   you. ___
(Recite) I ___   stop rhythm

pp

Killing Me Softly With His Song

Words by Norman Gimbel | Music by Charles Fox

Voice: clarinet
Rhythm: bossa nova
Tempo: medium (♩ = 104)

VERSES

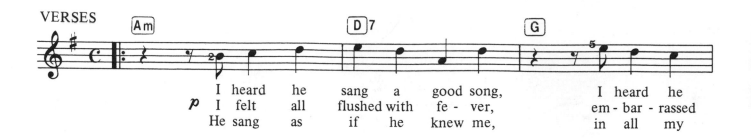

I heard he sang a good song, I heard he
I felt all flushed with fe - ver,
He sang as if he knew me, in all my

had a style. And so I came to see him, and
by the crowd. I felt he found my let - ters, and
dark des - pair. And then he looked right through me, as

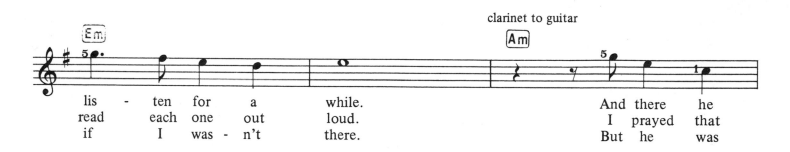

clarinet to guitar

lis - ten for a while. And there he
read each one out loud. I prayed that
if I was - n't there. But he was

cross over thumb   new hand position

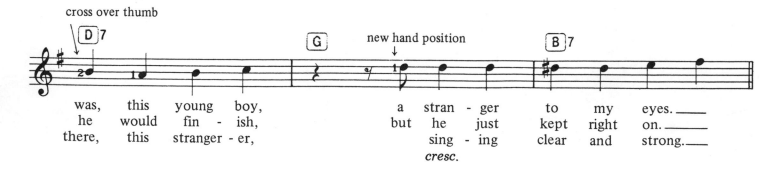

was, this young boy, a stran - ger to my eyes. ___
he would fin - ish, but he just kept right on. ___
there, this stranger - er, sing - ing clear and strong. ___
cresc.

CHORUS

Strum-ming my pain ___ with his fin - gers, ___ sing - ing my life ___ with his
f

words. Killing me soft - ly with his song, kill - ing me soft -

mf dim.

- ly with his song, tell - ing my whole ___ life with

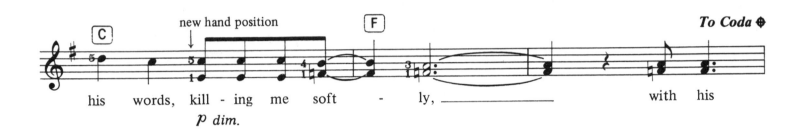

his words, kill - ing me soft - ly, ___ with his

p dim.

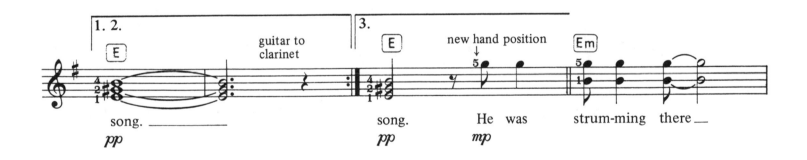

song. ___ song. He was strum - ming there ___

pp *pp* *mp*

yea, he was sing - ing my life.

Kill - ing me soft - ly with

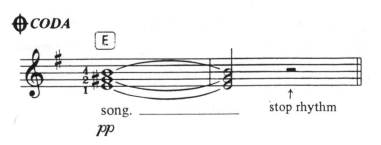

song. ___

pp

stop rhythm

Love Is All Around

Words & Music by Reg Presley

Voice: brass ensemble
Rhythm: rock
Tempo: medium (♩ = 92)

INTRO

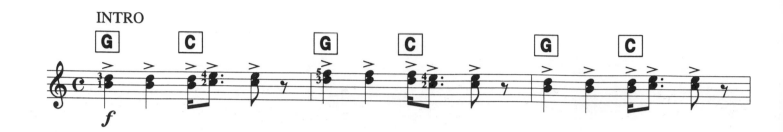

VERSES

1. I feel it in my fin - gers, I feel it in my toes.
mp (2.) see your face be - fore me, as I lay on my bed.

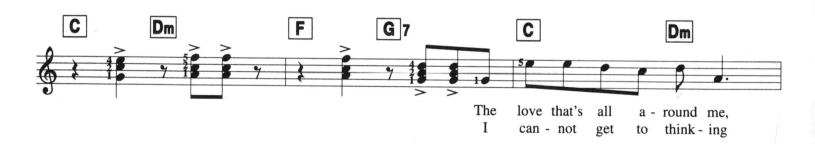

The love that's all a - round me,
I can - not get to think - ing

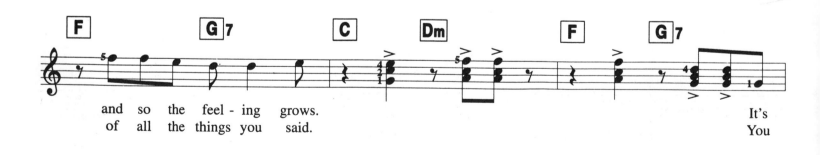

and so the feel - ing grows. It's
of all the things you said. You

writ - ten on the wind, it's ev - 'ry - where I go.
gave your pro - mise to me, and I gave mine to you.

So if you real - ly love me, come on and let it show.
I need some - one be - side me in ev - 'ry - thing I do.

INTERLUDE

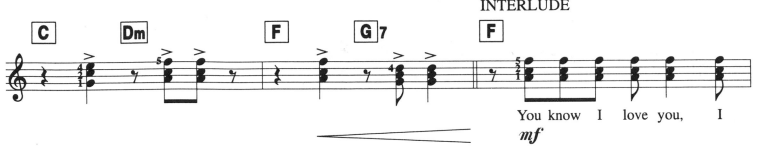

You know I love you, I
mf

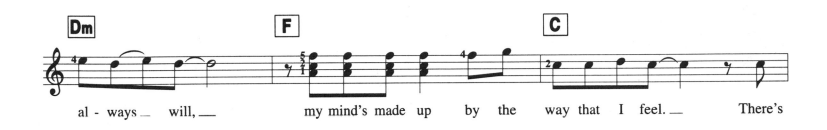

al - ways will, my mind's made up by the way that I feel. There's

no be - gin - ning, there'll be no end, 'cause

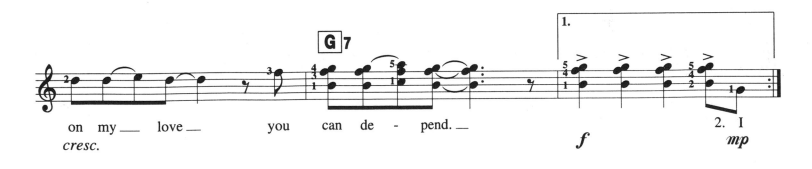

1.

on my love you can de - pend.
cresc. *f* 2. I *mp*

2.

D.%. and fade

Got to keep it mo - ving!
f 1. I *mp*

LOVE SHINE A LIGHT

WORDS & MUSIC BY KIMBERLEY REW

Voice: vibraphone
Rhythm: rock
Tempo: medium (♩ = 96)

VERSE

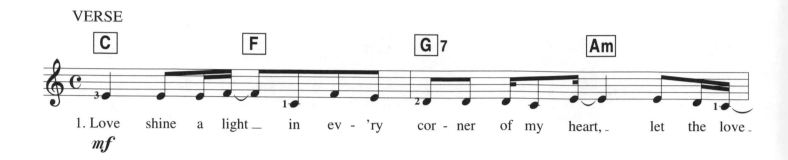

1. Love shine a light __ in ev - 'ry cor - ner of my heart, __ let the love __

mf

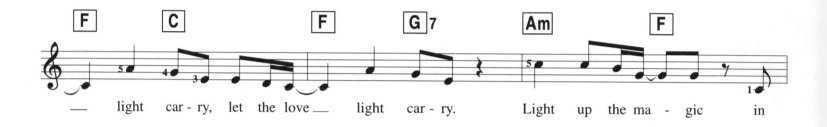

__ light car - ry, let the love __ light car - ry. Light up the ma - gic in

vibes to brass ensemble

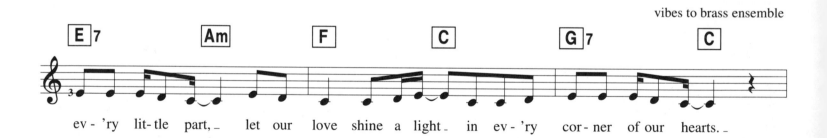

ev - 'ry lit - tle part, __ let our love shine a light __ in ev - 'ry cor - ner of our hearts. __

INSTRUMENTAL

brass to vibes

f

VERSES

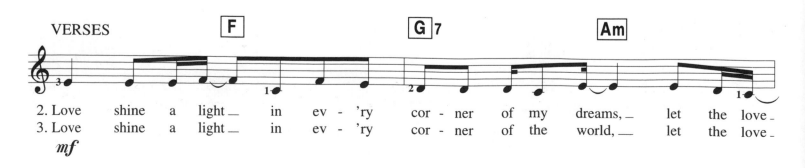

2. Love shine a light __ in ev - 'ry cor - ner of my dreams, __ let the love __
3. Love shine a light __ in ev - 'ry cor - ner of the world, __ let the love __

mf

MORE THAN I CAN SAY
WORDS & MUSIC BY SONNY CURTIS & JERRY ALLISON

Voice: guitar
Rhythm: rock
Tempo: medium (♩ = 112)

Oh,___ oh,___ yea,___ yea!___ I love you more than I___ can

say.___ I'll love you twice as much to - mor - row,___ oh,___

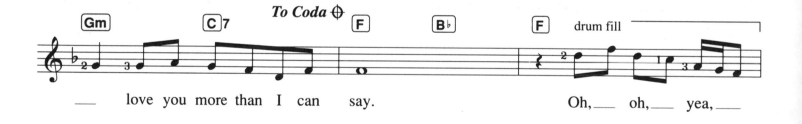

___ love you more than I can say. Oh,___ oh,___ yea,___

yea!___ I miss you ev - 'ry sin - gle day.___

Why must my life be filled with sor - row?___ Oh,___ love you more than I can

say.

mp

Don't you know I need you   so?_____

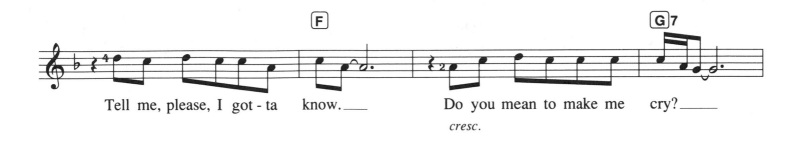

Tell me, please, I got - ta   know.___   Do you mean to make me   cry?_____

cresc.

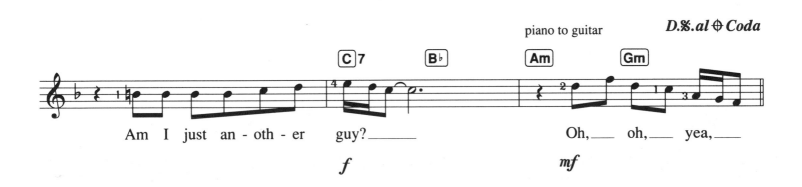

piano to guitar

D.%.al ⊕ Coda

Am I just an - oth - er   guy?_____   Oh,___ oh,___ yea,___

f   *mf*

⊕ **CODA**

say.   I love you more than I can   say.

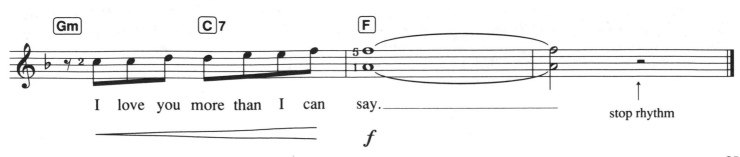

I love you more than I can   say._____

stop rhythm

f

ONE SWEET DAY

WORDS & MUSIC BY MARIAH CAREY, WALTER AFANASIEFF, SHAWN STOCKMAN,
MICHAEL MCCARY, NATHAN MORRIS & WANYA MORRIS

Voice: piano
Rhythm: 8 beat
Tempo: slow (♩ = 88)

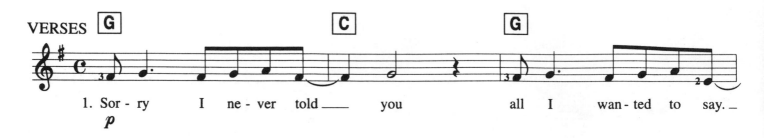

VERSES

1. Sor - ry I ne - ver told ___ you all I wan - ted to say. ___
p

___ And now it's too late to hold ___ you, 'cause

you've flown a - way, so far a - way. ___ 2. Ne - ver, had I i - mag-
mf   *p*

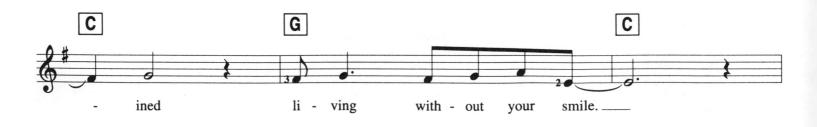

- ined li - ving with - out your smile. ___

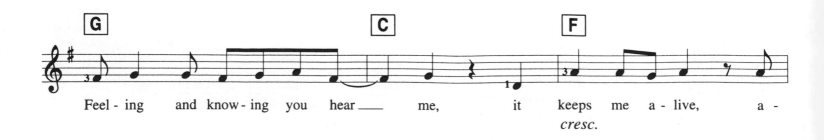

Feel - ing and know - ing you hear ___ me, it keeps me a - live, a -
cresc.

CHORUS

live. _____ And I know you're shi-ning down on me from Hea-ven, like so

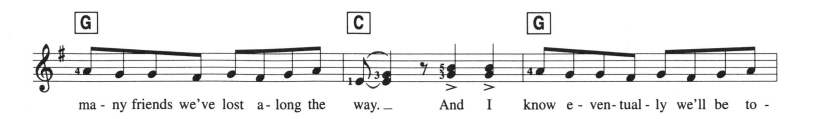

ma-ny friends we've lost a-long the way. __ And I know e-ven-tual-ly we'll be to-

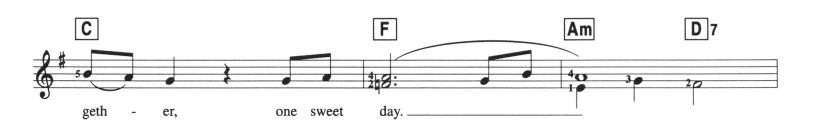

geth - er, one sweet day. _____

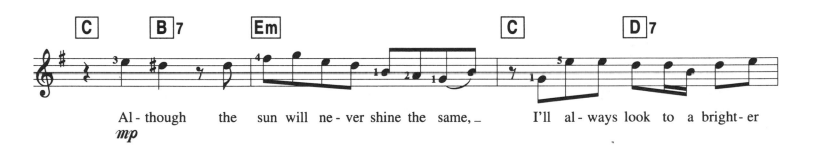

Al-though the sun will ne-ver shine the same, _ I'll al-ways look to a bright-er

day. _____ Lord, I know _ when I __ lay me down to sleep, _

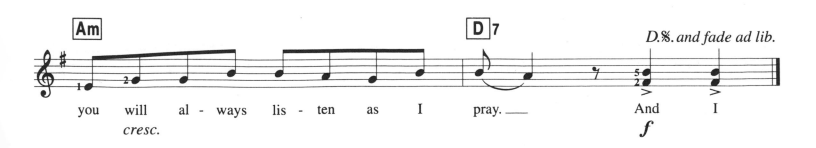

you will al-ways lis-ten as I pray. ___ And I

33

Say You'll Be There

WORDS & MUSIC BY ELIOT KENNEDY, JON B, VICTORIA AADAMS, MELANIE BROWN, EMMA BUNTON, MELANIE CHISHOLM & GERI HALLIWELL

Voice: human voice
Rhythm: 8 beat
Tempo: medium ($\quarternote$ = 108)

VERSES

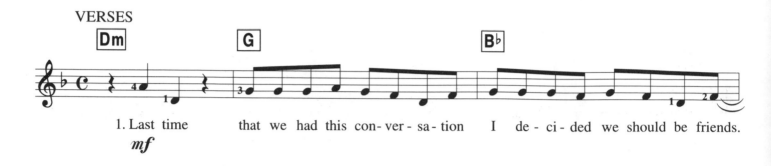

1. Last time that we had this con-ver-sa-tion I de-ci-ded we should be friends.

——— Yeah! But now we're go-ing 'round in cir-cles, tell me,

will this dé-jà vu ne-ver end? ___ Oh! 2. Now you tell me that you've
3. If you put two and

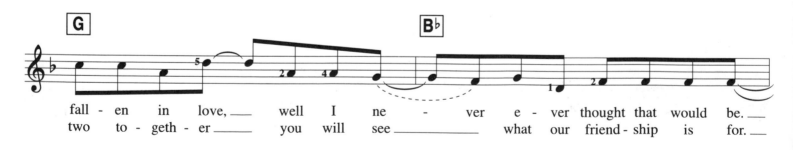

fall-en in love, ___ well I ne-ver e-ver thought that would be. ___
two to-geth-er _____ you will see _____ what our friend-ship is for. ___

——————— Yeah! This time you got-ta take it ea-sy, throw-ing
If you can't work out this e-qua-tion, then I'll

far too much e - mo - tion at me. ____ But a - ny fool ____ can see ____ they're fall -
guess I'll have to show you the door. ____ There is no need ____ to say ____ you love ____

- ing, I got - ta make you un - der - stand. _____
____ me, it would be bet - ter left ____ un - said. _____

cresc.

CHORUS

I'm giv - ing you ev - 'ry - thing, ___ all that joy ____ can bring, ___ this I swear.

f

_____ And all that I want ____ from you ____ is a pro -

1.

- mise you ____ will be there. ____ Say you will ____ be there, _____ oh,

2.

cut flute   D.%. *and fade*

say you will be there. Won't you sing it with me? ____

Stereotypes

Words & Music by Damon Albarn, Graham Coxon, Alex James & David Rowntree

Voice: jazz organ, with chorale (chorus)
Rhythm: rock
Tempo: medium (♩ = 112)

VERSES

1. The sub-urbs they are dream-ing, they're a twin-kle in her eye,
(2.) sub-urbs they are sleep-ing, but he's dress-ing up to-night, She

she's been feel-ing fris-ky since her hus-band said good-bye. She
likes a man in un-i-form, he loves to wear it tight. They are

wears a low cut T-shirt, runs a lit-tle B and B, she's
on the lov-er's so-fa, they are on the pa-ti-o, and

most ac-com-mo-da-ting when she's in her lin-ge-rie. Wife
when the fun is o-ver, watch them-selves on vi-de-o. The

swap-ping is the fu-ture, you know that it would suit you!
neigh-bours may be star-ing, but they are just past ca-ring.

tremolo on

CHORUS

Yes, _____ _____ they're ste - re - o - types, _____ there must be more to

life. All your life you're dream - ing, _____ and then you stop dream - ing, from

time to time you know you should be go - ing on an - o - ther ben - der.

2. The

Yes, _____

_____ there must be more to life than ste - re - o - types. _____

Wife swap - ping is the fu - ture, you know that it would suit you!

37

Tears In Heaven

WORDS & MUSIC BY ERIC CLAPTON & WILL JENNINGS

Voice: horn
Rhythm: 8 beat
Tempo: medium (♩ = 88)

VERSES

1. Would you know my name, _____ if I saw you in hea-ven?
2. Would you hold my hand, _____ if I saw you in hea-ven?

Would you be the same, _____
Would you help me stand, _____

if I saw you in hea-ven? I must be strong,
if I saw you in hea-ven? I'll find my way

and car-ry on. _____ 'Cause I
through night and day. _____ 'Cause I

know I don't be-long _____ here in hea-ven.
know I just can't stay _____ here in hea-ven.

INTERLUDE

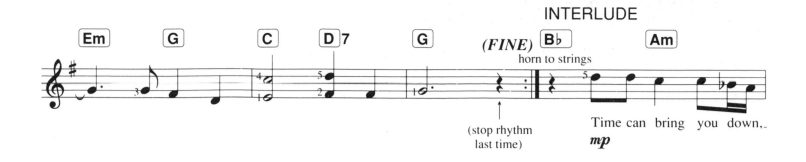

(FINE)

horn to strings

(stop rhythm last time)

Time can bring you down,
mp

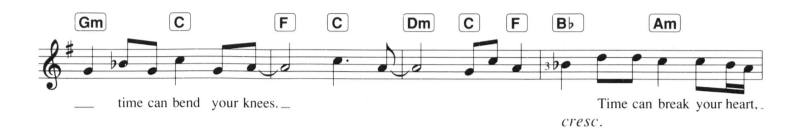

time can bend your knees. Time can break your heart,
cresc.

D.C. (VERSES 3. & 4.) al FINE

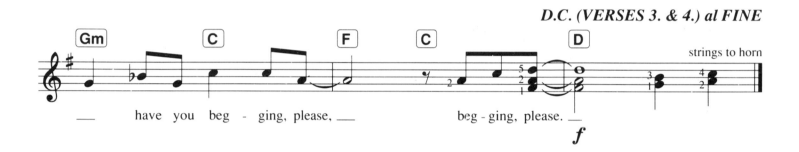

strings to horn

have you beg - ging, please, beg - ging, please.
f

VERSE 3

INSTRUMENTAL *(first 8 bars)*

Beyond the door
There's peace, I'm sure.
And I know there'll be no more
Tears in heaven.

VERSE 4

Would you know my name
If I saw you in heaven?
Would you be the same
If I saw you in heaven?
I must be strong
And carry on,
'Cause I know I don't belong
Here in heaven.

THINK TWICE

WORDS & MUSIC BY ANDY HILL & PETE SINFIELD

Voice: human voice
Rhythm: 8 beat
Tempo: slow (♩ = 76)

VERSE

Don't think I can't feel that there's some - thing wrong. —

You've been the sweet-est part of my life for so long. — I look in your eyes, there's a

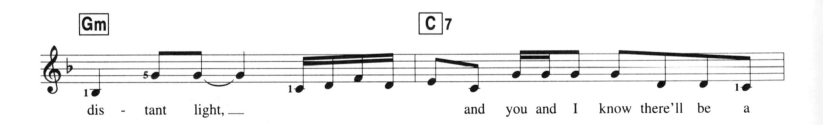

dis - tant light, — and you and I know there'll be a

storm to - night. _____ This is get - ting se - ri - ous.

CHORUS

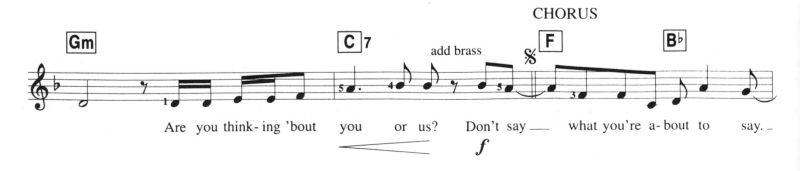

Are you think-ing 'bout you or us? Don't say ___ what you're a-bout to say. —

40

Look back ___ be - fore you leave my life. Be sure ___

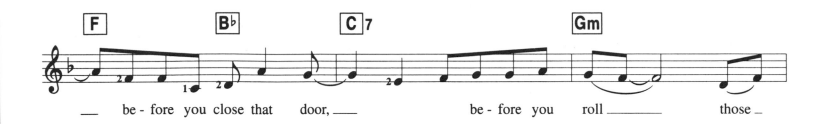

___ be - fore you close that door, ___ be - fore you roll ___ those ___

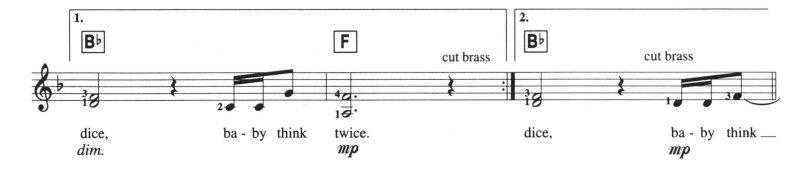

1.

dice, ba - by think twice.
dim. *mp*

2.

dice, ba - by think ___
mp

BRIDGE

twice.

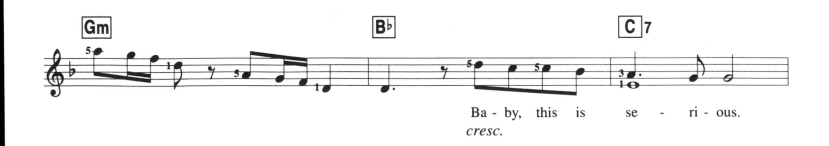

Ba - by, this is se - ri - ous.
cresc.

Are you think - ing 'bout you ___ or us? ___ Ba - by, ___ don't say ___
f

TIME TO SAY GOODBYE

WORDS & MUSIC BY F. SARTORI & L. QUARANTOTTO | ADAPTED BY FRANK PETERSON

Voice: clarinet
Rhythm: 8 beat
Tempo: slow (♩ = 69)

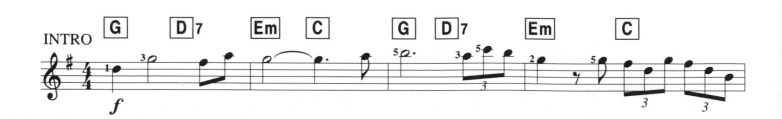

Quan- do so- no so- lo so- gno l'o- riz- zon- te man- can le par -

ro - le, si lo so che non c'é lu - ce u - na stan- za quan- do man- ca

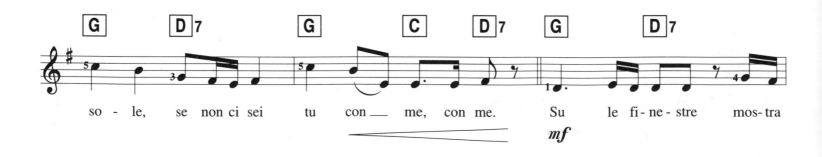

so - le, se non ci sei tu con ___ me, con me. Su le fi- ne- stre mos- tra

tutti il mio cu- ore che hai ac- ce- so. chiu- di – den- tro me la lu- ce

CHORUS

che - hai con-tra-to per stra-da. Time to say good-bye, pa - e - si___ che non ho

mai, ve-du-to vis-su-to con me, a-des-so si, li vi-vrò con te, par-ti-

rò su na-vi per ma-ri___ che io lo so, no, no, non e-si-sto-no

VERSE

più, it's time to say good-bye. Quan-do sei lon-ta-na sog-no l'o-riz-zon-te man-can le pa-

ro - le. E io si, lo so che sei con me, con me, tu mia lu-na, tu sei qui con me

D.%.al Coda

mi - o so - le tu sei qui con me, con me, con me, con me.

⊕ **Coda**

più, io con te.___

stop rhythm

Unchained Melody

WORDS BY HY ZARET | MUSIC BY ALEX NORTH

Voice: string ensemble
Rhythm: bossa nova
Tempo: medium (♩ = 116)

Oh,   my   love,   my   dar - ling,   I've
Time   goes   by   so   slow - ly,   and
mp

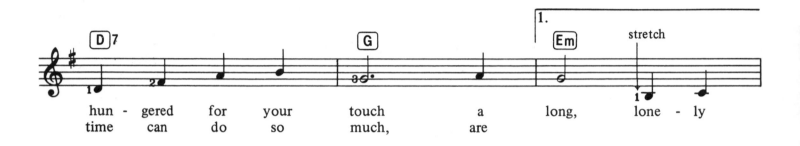

hun - gered   for   your   touch   a   long,   lone - ly
time   can   do   so   much,   are

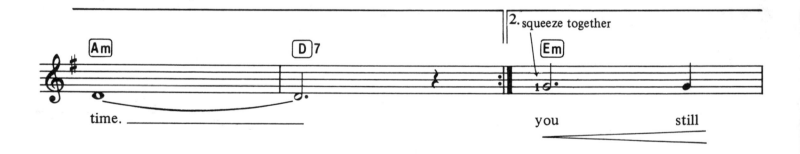

time. _____   you   still

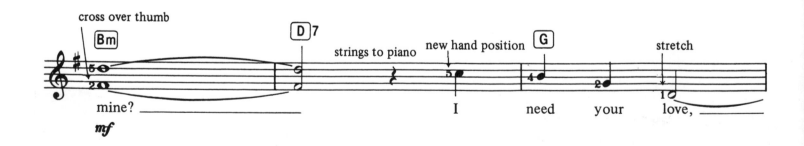

cross over thumb
mine? _____   I   need   your   love, _____
mf
strings to piano   new hand position   stretch

_____   I   need   your   love, _____   God

44

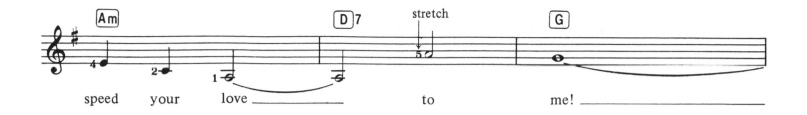

speed   your   love _____ to   me! _____

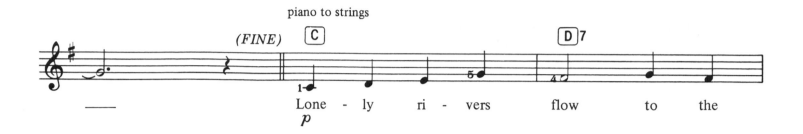

_____ Lone - ly   ri - vers   flow   to   the

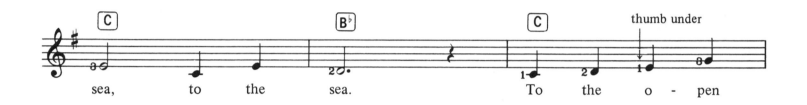

sea,   to   the   sea.   To   the   o - pen

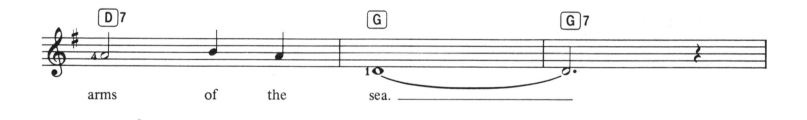

arms   of   the   sea. _____

Lone - ly   ri - vers   sigh: "Wait   for   me,   wait   for   me!"

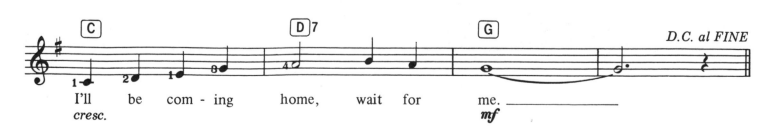

I'll   be   com - ing   home,   wait   for   me. _____

WHEN YOU TELL ME THAT YOU LOVE ME

WORDS & MUSIC BY ALBERT HAMMOND & JOHN BETTIS

Voice: oboe
Rhythm: 8 beat
Tempo: medium (♩ = 92)

WHY

WORDS & MUSIC BY ANNIE LENNOX

Voice: human voice
Rhythm: 8 beat
Tempo: medium (♩ = 104)

CHORUS

Why?

Why?

VERSE

human voice to piano

How ma-ny times ___

___ do I have to try to tell you that I'm ___ sor-ry for the things ___

___ I've done. ___   Ooh. ___

But when I start to try to tell you, that's when you have to tell me,

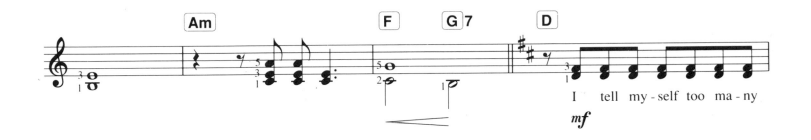
hey, this kind of _____ trou-ble's on - ly just _____ be - gun.

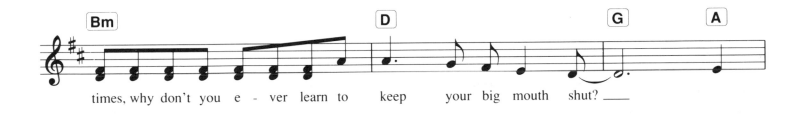
I tell my-self too ma - ny

times, why don't you e - ver learn to keep your big mouth shut? _____

That's why it hurts so bad to hear the words that keep on _____ fall - ing from your mouth, _____

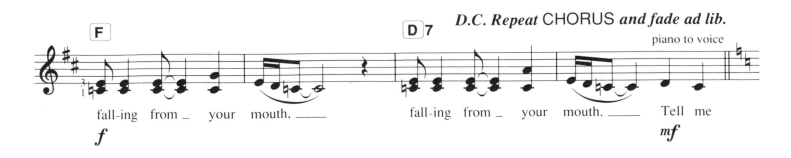

D.C. Repeat CHORUS *and fade ad lib.*

piano to voice

fall-ing from _ your mouth, _____ fall-ing from _ your mouth. _____ Tell me

f   *mf*

WILD WOOD
WORDS & MUSIC BY PAUL WELLER

Voice: clarinet
Rhythm: 8 beat
Tempo: fast (♩ =152)

VERSES

1. High   tide, _____   mid - af - ter - noon, _____
2. Don't   let _____   them get you down, _____
mp

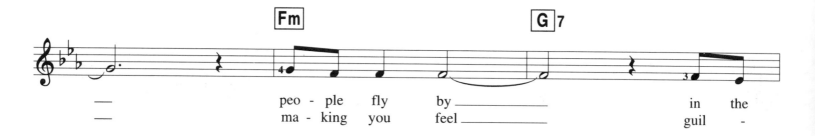

— peo - ple fly by _____ in the
— ma - king you feel _____ guil -

traff - ic's   boom. _____   know   -   ing _____
ty   a   -   bout _____   gold - en rain _____

— just where you're blow - ing, _____
— will bring you rich - - es, _____

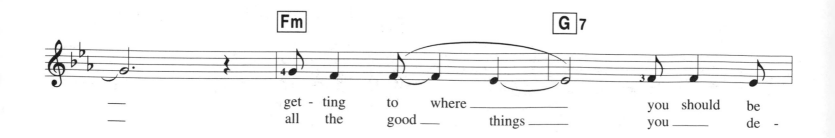

— get - ting   to where _____   you should be
— all the good ___ things _____   you _____ de -

50

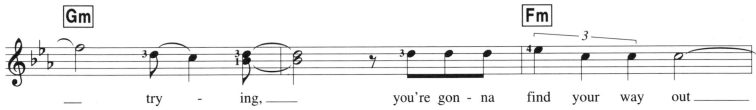

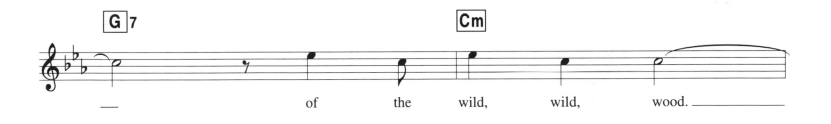

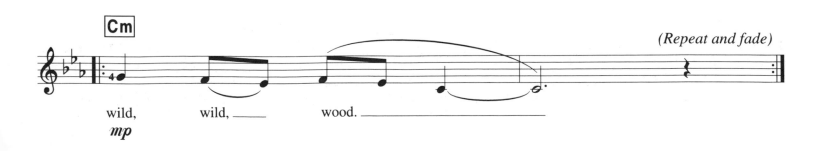

Without You

WORDS & MUSIC BY PETER HAM & TOM EVANS

Voice: vibes
Rhythm: rock
Tempo: slow (♩ = 76)

Verse

No, I can't for-get this ev-'ning, or your face as you were leav-ing, but I

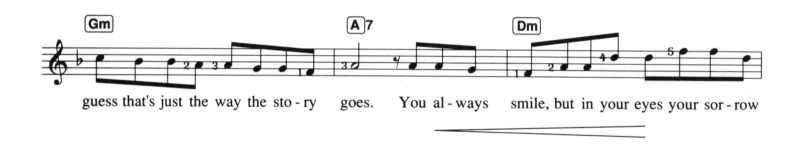

guess that's just the way the sto-ry goes. You al-ways smile, but in your eyes your sor-row

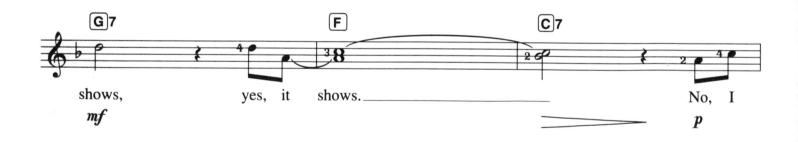

shows, yes, it shows._____ No, I

can't for-get to-mor-row when I think of all my sor-row, and I had you there, but then I let you

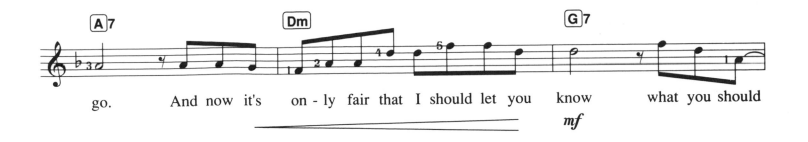

go.   And now it's   on - ly fair that I should let you   know   what you should

mf

vibes to
string ensemble

CHORUS

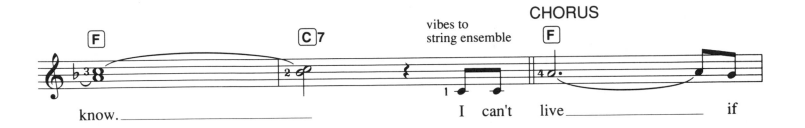

know. _____   I   can't   live _____   if

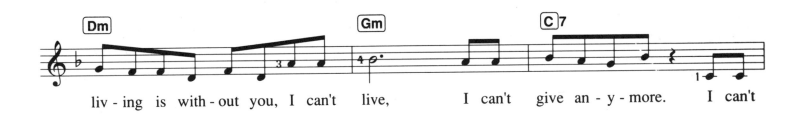

liv - ing is with - out you, I can't   live,   I can't   give an - y - more.   I can't

live _____   if   liv - ing is with - out you, I can't   give,   I can't

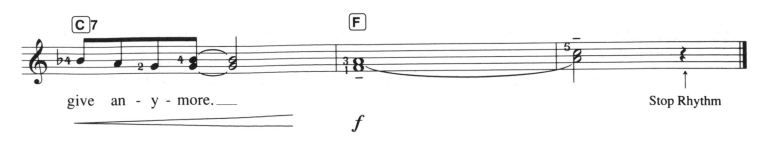

give an - y - more. _____   Stop Rhythm

f

WONDERFUL TONIGHT

WORDS & MUSIC BY ERIC CLAPTON

Voice: guitar
Rhythm: rock
Tempo: medium (♩ = 108)

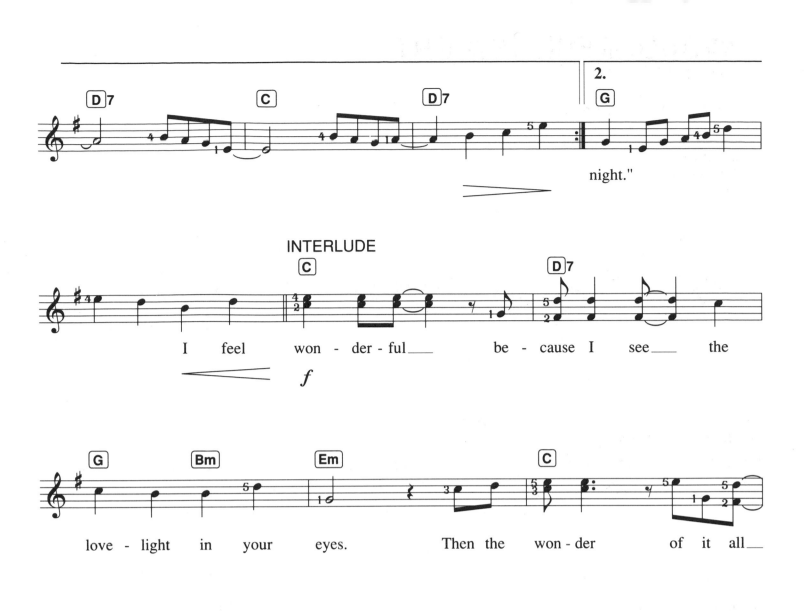

night."

INTERLUDE

I feel won - der - ful___ be - cause I see___ the

f

love - light in your eyes. Then the won - der of it all__

__ is that you just don't re - a - lize how much__ I

love you. *dim.*

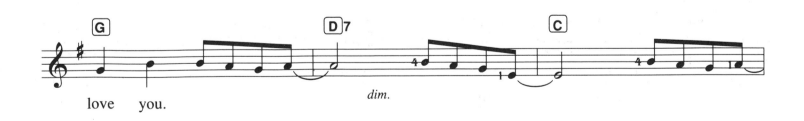

D.C. al ⊕ Coda

⊕ *CODA*

electric piano
to guitar

night."

stop rhythm

You Are Not Alone

WORDS & MUSIC BY ROBERT KELLY

Voice: human voice
Rhythm: 8 beat
Tempo: very slow (♩ = 63)

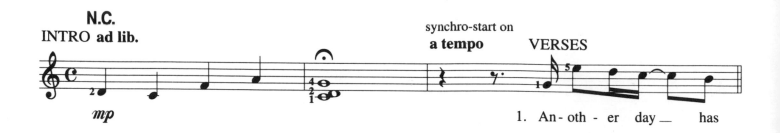

1. An-oth-er day ___ has

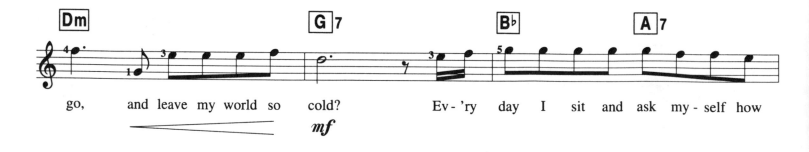

gone, I'm still all ___ a - lone. How could this be? You're not here with

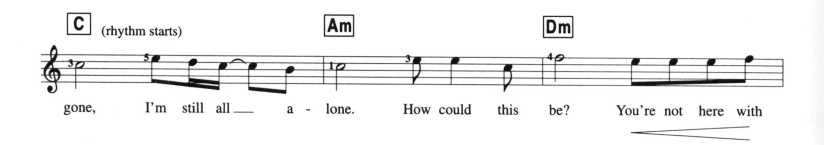

me. You ne-ver said ___ good-bye, some-one tell ___ me why did she have to

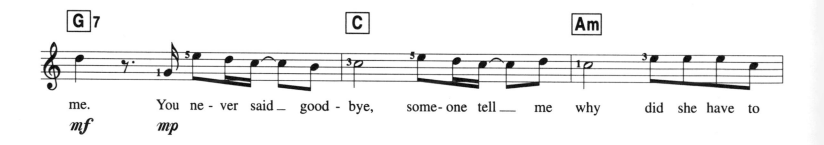

go, and leave my world so cold? Ev-'ry day I sit and ask my-self how

did this thing end? ___ Some-thing whis-pers in my ear and says: 2. You are not ___ a -

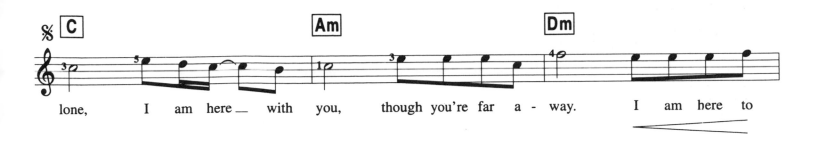

lone, I am here — with you, though you're far a - way. I am here to

stay. You are not — a - lone, I am here — with you though we're far a -
mf   *mp*

part, you're al - ways in my heart, but you are not — a - lone. (Fine)
f   (stop rhythm last time)

BRIDGE

add flute

Whis - per three words then I'll come run - ning, I ——
mp   *cresc.*

cut flute   *D.%.al Fine*

and girl you know that I'll be there, I'll be there. You are not — a -
f   *mp*

You Must Love Me

Music by Andrew Lloyd Webber | Lyrics by Tim Rice

Voice: oboe
Rhythm: 8 beat
Tempo: medium (♩ = 92)

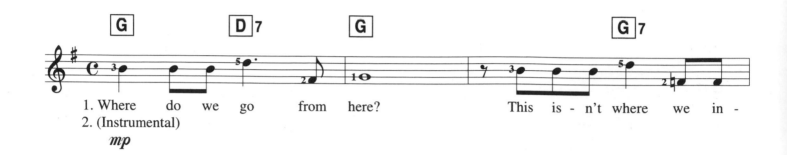

1. Where do we go from here? This is - n't where we in -
2. (Instrumental)
mp

ten - ded to be. __ We had it all, __ you be - lieved __ in me, __ I be -
cresc.

lieved __ in you. __   *dim.*   Cer - tain - ties   dis - ap -
mf   (Vocal) Why are you   at my
                                   mp

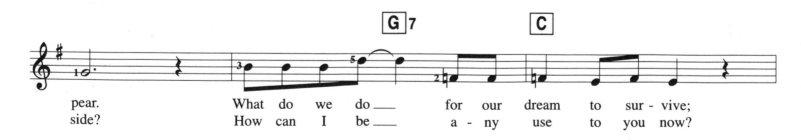

pear.   What do we do __ for our dream to sur - vive;
side?   How can I be __ a - ny use to you now?

how do we keep __ all our pas - sions a - live, __   as
Give me a chance, __ and I'll let you see how __
cresc.

58

Common People

MUSIC BY PULP | LYRICS BY JARVIS COCKER

Voice: guitar
Rhythm: rock
Tempo: medium (♩ = 112)

VERSES

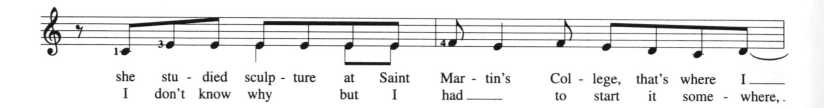

1. She came from Greece, she had a thirst for know - ledge,
2. I took her to a su - per - mar - ket,

mf

she stu - died sculp - ture at Saint Mar - tin's Col - lege, that's where I ___
I don't know why but I had ___ to start it some - where,

___ caught her eye. ___
___ so ___ it start - ed there.

She told me that her dad was load - ed,
I said, "Pre - tend you've got no mo - ney,"

I said, "In that case I'll have rum and Co - ca Co - la," she said. "Fine." ___
but she just laughed and said, "Oh you're so fun - ny," I said,

BRIDGE

flat a-bove a shop, — cut your hair, and get a job. — Smoke some

fags, and play — some pool, — pre-tend you ne-ver went — to school. — But still you

ne-ver get it right, — cos when you're laid in bed at night, — watch-ing

roa-ches climb — the wall, — if you called your dad, he could stop
cresc.

D.%.al Coda **Coda**

— it all, yeah! you'll ne-ver watch your life — slide out of view,
f

— and dance, and drink, — and screw, — be-cause there's

no-thing else — to do." — stop rhythm

62

CHORD CHARTS (For Left Hand)

C

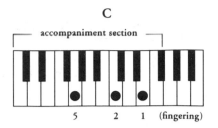

5   2   1   (fingering)

Cm

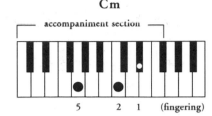

5   2   1   (fingering)

C7

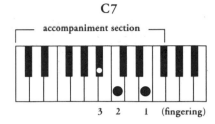

3   2   1   (fingering)

D♭

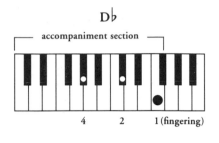

4   2   1 (fingering)

C♯m

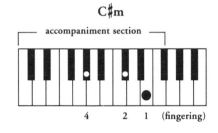

4   2   1   (fingering)

D♭(C♯)7

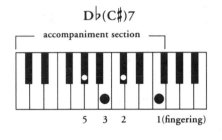

5   3   2   1(fingering)

D

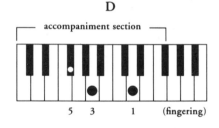

5   3   1   (fingering)

Dm

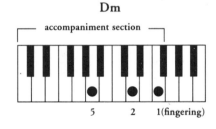

5   2   1(fingering)

D7

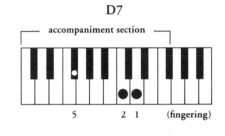

5   2 1   (fingering)

E♭

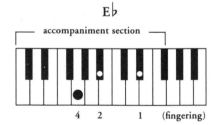

4   2   1   (fingering)

E♭m

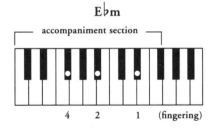

4   2   1   (fingering)

E♭7

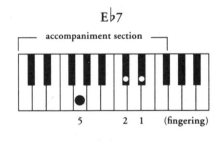

5   2 1   (fingering)

E

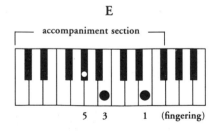

5   3   1   (fingering)

Em

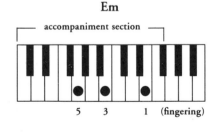

5   3   1   (fingering)

E7

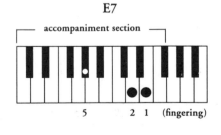

5   2 1   (fingering)

F

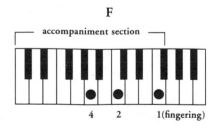

4   2   1(fingering)

Fm

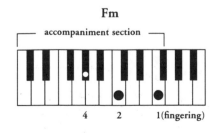

4   2   1(fingering)

F7

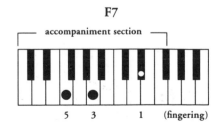

5   3   1   (fingering)

CHORD CHARTS (For Left Hand)

G♭(F♯)
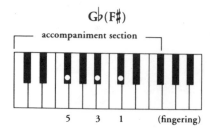
accompaniment section
5   3   1   (fingering)

F♯m
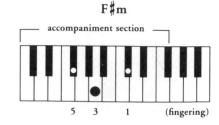
accompaniment section
5   3   1   (fingering)

G♭(F♯)7
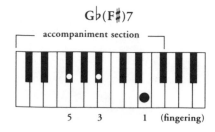
accompaniment section
5   3   1   (fingering)

G
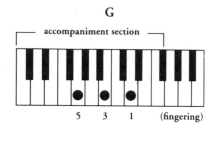
accompaniment section
5   3   1   (fingering)

Gm
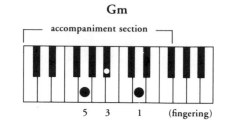
accompaniment section
5   3   1   (fingering)

G7
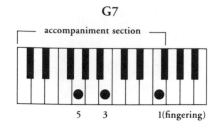
accompaniment section
5   3   1(fingering)

A♭
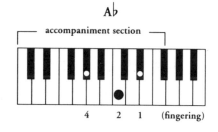
accompaniment section
4   2   1   (fingering)

A♭m
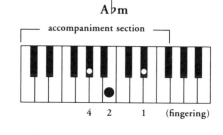
accompaniment section
4   2   1   (fingering)

A♭7
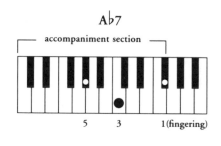
accompaniment section
5   3   1(fingering)

A
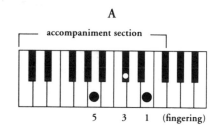
accompaniment section
5   3   1   (fingering)

Am
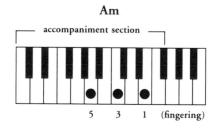
accompaniment section
5   3   1   (fingering)

A7
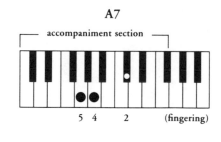
accompaniment section
5   4   2   (fingering)

B♭
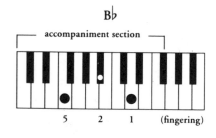
accompaniment section
5   2   1   (fingering)

B♭m
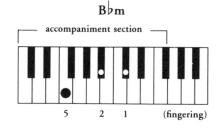
accompaniment section
5   2   1   (fingering)

B♭7
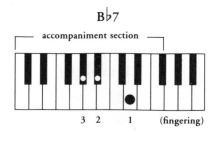
accompaniment section
3   2   1   (fingering)

B
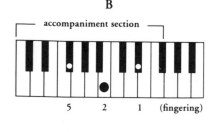
accompaniment section
5   2   1   (fingering)

Bm
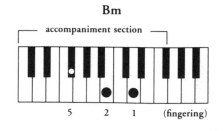
accompaniment section
5   2   1   (fingering)

B7
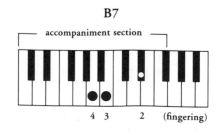
accompaniment section
4   3   2   (fingering)